WEST CROYDON TO EPSOM

Vic Mitchell and Keith Smith

First published November 1992

ISBN 1 873793 08 1

© Middleton Press 1992

Typesetting — Barbara Mitchell
Design — Deborah Goodridge

Published by Middleton Press
Easebourne Lane
Midhurst
West Sussex
GU29 9AZ
Tel: (0730) 813169

Printed & bound by Biddles Ltd,
Guildford and Kings Lynn

CONTENTS

ACKNOWLEDGEMENTS

We are extremely grateful for so much help given by many of those mentioned in the photographic credits. In addition, we express our gratitude to R.Carpenter, R.M.Casserley, Dr.E.Course, G.Gartside, G.Groughton, N.Langridge, A.Ll.Lambert, D.Pocock, R.Randell, D.Salter, N.Sprinks, N.Stanyon, Miss M.Wheeller and our ever helpful wives.

INDEX

L. B. & S. C. Ry.
Available on the DATE of issue ONLY.
SEE CONDITIONS AT BACK.
EPSOM TOWN
TO
London Bridge lb.
1s. 2d.   THIRD CL.   1s. 2d.
8197

Route map of 1955

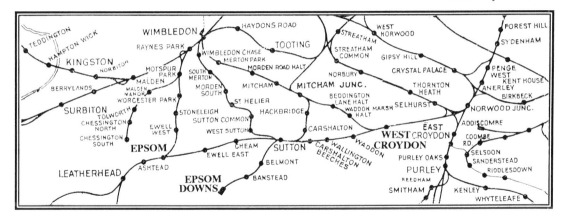

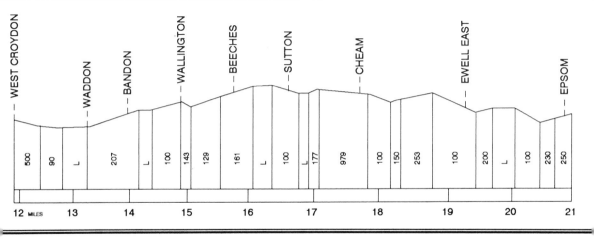

GEOGRAPHICAL SETTING

Almost all of the route runs on the chalk at the foot of the gentle dip slope of the North Downs, close to its boundary with the London Clay. Absence of rivers in this area resulted in few civil engineering structures being required.

The branch to Epsom Downs rises on this dip slope, a mile long cutting being required to cross Banstead Downs. The line climbs about 150ft in under four miles to the terminus, the land rising to 450ft above sea level south of the race course on Walton Downs.

The maps in this album are to the scale of 25" to 1 mile, unless otherwise shown.

HISTORICAL BACKGROUND

The London & Croydon Railway was opened on 5th June 1839 from London Bridge to the present West Croydon station. The London Brighton & South Coast Railway came into being in 1846 and extended the line to Epsom on 10th May 1847. An experiment with atmospheric propulsion was abandoned at this time. The branch from West Croydon to Wimbledon was opened on 22nd October 1855 and was operated by the LBSCR from 1856.

The Epsom to Wimbledon line was opened by the London & South Western Railway on 4th April 1859. The Epsom to Leatherhead section came into use in the same year but was jointly operated by the LBSCR and the LSWR.

The LBSCR opened two more lines in the Sutton area - to Epsom Downs on 22nd May 1865 and to Peckham Rye via Mitcham Junction on 1st October 1868. A third followed on 5th May 1930. This was to Wimbledon via St. Helier and was built by the Southern Railway. This company had come into being in 1923 and existed until 1948, when it became part of British Railways.

Electrification

The LBSCR chose an overhead conductor energised at 6700 volts AC for its suburban electrification programme which commenced in 1909. The advent of World War I caused delays, as a German equipment supplier had been chosen. It was not until 1st April 1925 that electric trains were running under the wires from Victoria to Sutton via West Croydon.

The SR opted for a third rail system, using 660 volts DC. Services commenced between London Bridge and Epsom Downs (via West Croydon) on 17th June 1928 and between Victoria and Epsom (via Mitcham Junction) on 3rd March 1929.

Overhead operation to Sutton ceased on 22nd September 1929 in the interests of standardisation.

PASSENGER SERVICES
Notes compiled by J.R.W.Kirkby

WEST CROYDON TO SUTTON

The initial 1847 service between London Bridge and Epsom consisted of 10 trains each way on weekdays and six on Sundays. Opening of the Balham - Windmill Bridge Junction line in 1862 brought trains from Victoria to Sutton via Thornton Heath and increasing traffic resulted, by the turn of the century, in 26 down and 24 up on weekdays. All but five started from London Bridge and ran to Sutton (15), Epsom (7) Epsom Downs (2) and Dorking (2).

Rail motor services were added in 1906, most running from West Croydon to stations on the Epsom Downs branch and by 1914 there were 20 daily. By this time trains were running to and from Wallington, where completion of the middle siding in 1916 allowed three suburban trains to be berthed overnight.

AC electrification between Victoria and Sutton via Thornton Heath in 1925 provided a 20 minute interval service for most of the day, supplemented by 24 steam services to and from

London Bridge, all but two rail motor services having ceased by then.

Three years later a London Bridge - Epsom Downs DC half-hourly electric service was introduced. By 1930, the Victoria - Sutton AC service had been converted to DC and extended to Epsom Downs. The new Wimbledon to Sutton line service between Holborn Viaduct and West Croydon meant the line enjoyed nine trains each way hourly at the peak, with six off peak, a state of affairs which lasted 37 years.

In 1992 there were four trains hourly (two from Victoria and two from London Bridge) and an off peak half-hourly Thameslink service between Luton and Guildford, calling only at West Croydon and Sutton.

Apart from summer extras, the route has rarely been used by main line trains except that between 1929 and 1938 a steam worked 10.10 am London Bridge to Portsmouth Harbour called at West Croydon and Sutton.

SUTTON TO EPSOM

The passenger service over this section was broadly the same as above until the opening of the Peckham Rye - Sutton section in 1868. The 1870 service consisted of 17 trains, all from London Bridge; to Epsom (4), Dorking (5), Horsham (3) and Brighton (5). Two of the Brighton trains did not call at Cheam or Ewell. Victoria trains at first did not go beyond Sutton.

The extent of traffic growth emerges from the 1914 total of 51 weekday down trains -

		From London Bridge	From Victoria
To	Cheam	6	7
	Epsom Town	11	9
	Dorking	6	1
	Holmwood	1	-
	Horsham	5	2
	Brighton	2	1
	Total	**31**	**20**

A number of local services omitted Ewell and a few both Cheam and Ewell.

Following electrification in 1929, two services, Victoria - Epsom and London Bridge to Effingham Junction or Dorking North (Horsham from 1938), each provided the usual 20-30 minute interval service. By 1992 only the Victoria service remained, running to Dorking North with additional trains to and from London Bridge at peak times, plus the off-peak Luton-Guildford Thameslink service which did not call at Cheam or Ewell East.

Main line trains between London and Portsmouth began to run via this route in 1871. The majority of trains used it from 1878 until 1978, when most were diverted to serve Gatwick Airport. None have used the Sutton route since 1984.

SUTTON TO EPSOM DOWNS

When the branch opened in 1865, there were eight trips each way and four on Sundays. This was soon halved, but by the turn of the century there were 14 services each way on weekdays and one or two ran to or from Victoria or London Bridge.

In 1906 a rail motor service started between West Croydon and Belmont. Within three years, apart from one or two peak trains, the branch was worked entirely by rail motors, involving 37 trips daily. By 1923 these had increased to 49, all three stations on the branch had become turn round points and some rail motor trips were extended to Crystal Palace, Mitcham and Wimbledon. Five different rail motors were involved daily.

Sunday services were withdrawn from the branch in 1868 and not restored until 1904. Under rail motor working, Sunday trains terminated at Banstead, except in the summer, but from 1914 there was again no Sunday service beyond Banstead until 1928.

From 1910 until 1928, two or three suburban trains ran from London to Banstead on Sunday afternoons for visitors to the several special hospitals close to Belmont and Banstead stations.

Electrification in 1928 resulted in an off peak service of four trains each way per hour, increased to six at peak times, half from London Bridge and half from Victoria and all normally running the full length of the branch.

The decline started in 1967 and now there is only an hourly service over a single line with one or two peak extras.

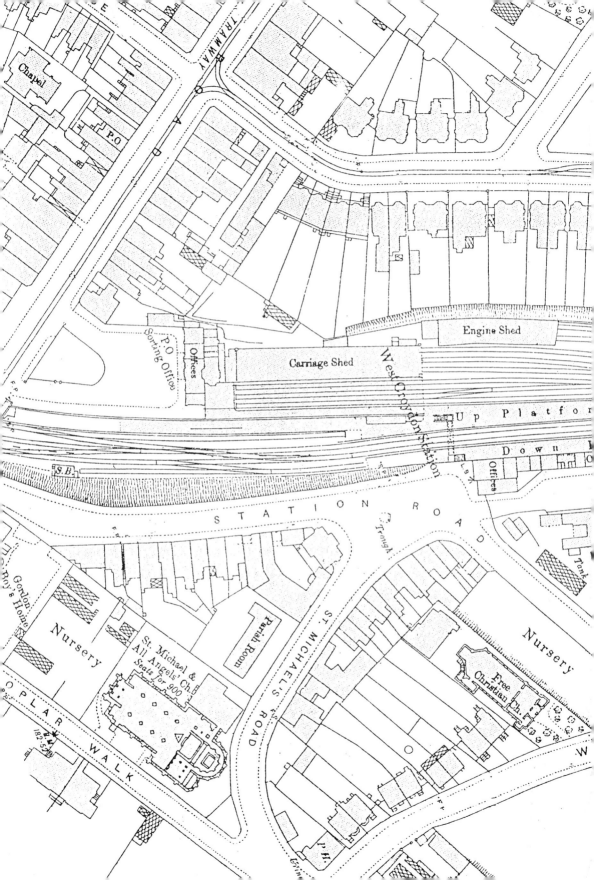

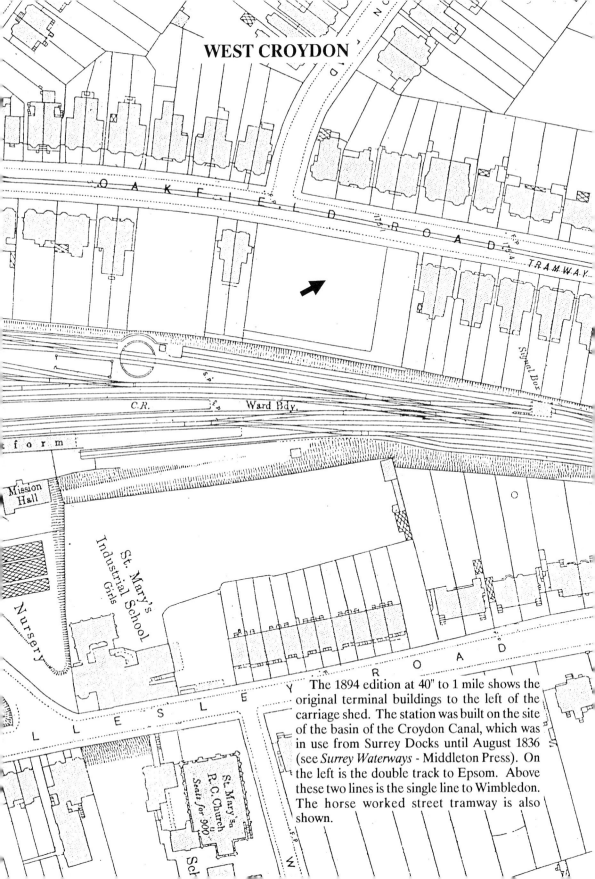

WEST CROYDON

O A K F E L D   R O A D

T R A M W A Y

Signal Box

C.R.   Ward Bdy.

f o r m

Mission Hall

St. Mary's Industrial School Girls

Nursery

L E S L E Y   R O A D

St. Mary's R.C. Church Seats for 900

The 1894 edition at 40" to 1 mile shows the original terminal buildings to the left of the carriage shed. The station was built on the site of the basin of the Croydon Canal, which was in use from Surrey Docks until August 1836 (see *Surrey Waterways* - Middleton Press). On the left is the double track to Epsom. Above these two lines is the single line to Wimbledon. The horse worked street tramway is also shown.

1. Viewed from the down platform is a D class 0-4-2T with a train of close coupled four-wheelers passing the elevated signal box and bound for the original terminal platform, which came into use on 5th June 1839. (R.C.Riley coll.)

2. Taking water at the down platform is class E4 no. 476 *Beeding*, showing the headcode for Portsmouth. This platform is on a falling gradient of 1 in 500 and was brought into use on 10th May 1847, the station having been a terminus for eight years. Initially named "Croydon", it became "Croydon Town" in May 1847 and "West Croydon" in April 1851. Local freight traffic was concentrated at East Croydon. (Lens of Sutton)

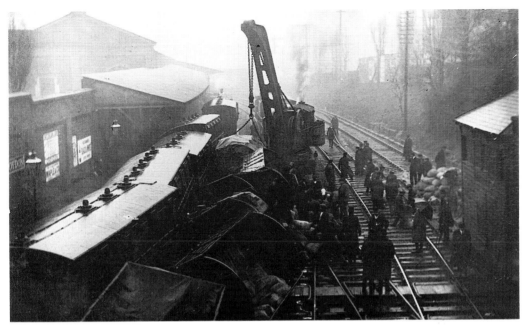

3. The scattered carriages are in the Wimbledon bay. On 4th July 1895 greasy rails caused a train terminating in this bay to collide with the buffer stops, but this is a later accident at the same location. On the left is the facade of the terminus, with South Box on the right. (Lens of Sutton)

4. The location of the engine shed (centre background) can be seen on the map, the roof on the left being that of the original terminus. On shed are E4X no. 466, E5 no. 404, D1 no. 273, D1 no. 243 and D3 no. 363. Note that only the up bay and adjacent siding were wired for electric trains. (J.R.W.Kirkby coll.)

5. Another view from the late 1920s includes the first station buildings and the electrification gantries. The two coaches are standing in a siding that was eliminated, when a separate goods line from Waddon Marsh was provided at the time of the electrification of the line to Wimbledon in 1930. (J.R.W.Kirkby coll.)

6. Seen from the up bay on 17th April 1927 are class D1 nos. B 282 and B 266, together with class E4 no. B 509 and two other locomotives allocated here for local passenger and freight work. In 1931 the prefix B was replaced by 2 on the "ex-Brighton" engines. (H.C.Casserley)

7. The terminal train shed and platform 1 are seen between the removal of overhead wiring in 1930 and the demolition of the roof in 1933. The loss of the gloomy structure was not mourned by many. A 3SUB electric set is on the left. (Lens of Sutton)

8. Engines were stabled here from 1839 until 1935. After the electrification of local passenger services about twelve locomotives were retained for freight work. Seen by the coal stage in June 1934 is class E4 no. 2484 and class E3 no. 2454, both with Westinghouse air pumps on their cab sides. (H.F.Wheeller)

July 1908

WEST CROYDON, BELMONT, and BANSTEAD (Motor Cars—One class only).—L. B. & S. C.			
Down.	**Week Days.**		**Sundays.**

(Timetable for West Croydon, Waddon, Wallington, Sutton, Belmont, Banstead and return, with numerous departure times — see original for full detail.)

a Runs 5 minutes later on Saturdays.   b Arrives at 8 41 mrn.   c Except Saturdays.   s Saturdays only.
** Banstead and Burgh Heath. †† Station for Beddington (¾ mile), Bandon Hill (1 mile) and Beddington Lane (2¼ miles).
¶¶ "Halts" at Bandon, between Waddon and Wallington; and Beeches, between Wallington and Sutton.

9. The shed closed in 1935 when the allocation was transferred to the new depot at Norwood Junction. The 46ft turntable had been taken out of use some years earlier. The stores train is ready to leave with the remaining equipment and material on 6th July 1935. (H.F.Wheeller)

10. The industries of the Wandle Valley demanded vast quantities of coal, notably for the production of gas and electricity. Class E6 no. 2417 is bound for Waddon Marsh on 12th September 1936. Above the two boys is the starting signal for Wimbledon electrics. Above the cab roof are the five steps up to platform 1, the up bay. (H.F.Wheeller)

11. The down side was subjected to enemy action on 9th October 1940 and, at about this time, first class accommodation was abolished on suburban services. The 3SUB in the background still carries a figure 3 on each door, a distinction soon removed. (British Rail)

1931 traffic	
Ordinary tickets issued	1,001,075
Season tickets issued	5,607
Platform tickets issued	21,600
Number of parcels	18,150
Number of milk churns	6,751

12. Towards the end of WWII, flying bombs (V1) and rockets (V2) caused great blast damage. The up platform was damaged and the end of a 3SUB was blown in on 23rd June 1944. (British Rail)

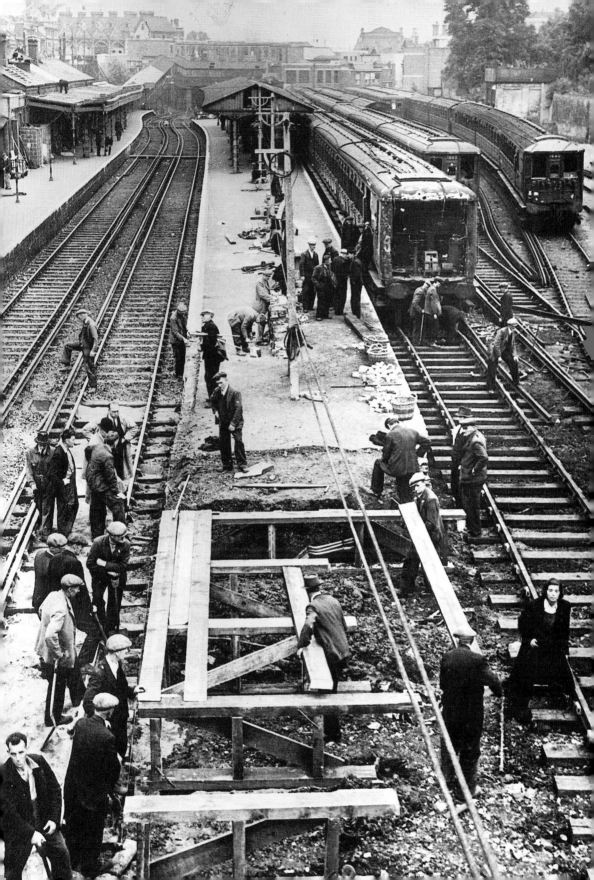

13. A 1948 northward view shows the Sutton lines on the right, the single line to Wimbledon left of centre and the goods line (and its associated ringed signals) on the left. The rebuilding in 1933-34 included the widening of London Road bridge to accommodate shops, the backs of which are evident here. A new booking office and single street-level entrance were provided. (British Rail)

14. Seen in 1954 are the four electrified berthing sidings laid out on the sites of the former terminus and carriage shed. A fifth was provided under "A" box and was the only one to remain in 1992, although seldom used. Unit no. 4126 failed to stop at platform 1 in about 1949 and crashed into vehicles in the car park. (D.Cullum)

15. "B" Box had its pitched roof removed in 1933 to allow girders to be erected to support new shops in Station Road. The box was photographed in 1972 and closed on 18th October 1981. (E.Wilmshurst)

16. Following closure of "B" box, a new connection to the Wimbledon line (left) was brought into use. It is remote from the station and carries no regular passenger service. 4SUB no.4721 is working the 17.10 Victoria to Sutton on 21st July 1983. The last of these units was withdrawn in the following October, although one was preserved - see picture 52. (J.Scrace)

17. There was a mixture of semaphore and colour light signals from 1954 until 8th April 1984 when "A" Box (background) was closed. The Victoria panel at Clapham Junction took control of the area. 4EPB no.5420 is seen leaving platform 1 for Victoria in the previous January. (F.Hornby)

18. The redundant down side buildings were still standing in 1992. The coming of the railways to this small market town resulted in phenomenal growth. Population (in 1000s) increased thus: 1841 - 16, 1861 - 30, 1887 - 78, 1901 - 134 and 1964 - 253. (J.Scrace)

Other pictures of West Croydon appear in a companion album in this series, *Mitcham Junction Lines.*

L. B & S. C. E. L. & Metropolitan Rys.
Available on the Date of issue **ONLY.**
This ticket is issued subject to the Regulations & Conditions stated in the Joint Companies Time Tables & Bills.

0065 0065

5900 5900

WEST CROYDON
TO
LIVERPOOL STREET [MET
Via New Cross & Metropolitan Ry.
10d.   THIRD CLASS   10d.

19. The footbridge from which this photograph was taken in 1991 was completed in 1934 and replaced the often-flooded subway marked on the map. The Wimbledon bay (left), out of line and at a lower level to the other bay platform, gives this historic station a unique character. (J.Scrace)

WADDON

20. This northward view includes tramway standards and so was taken after 1906, when electric trams commenced to operate between Croydon and Sutton. Sheaves of corn in stooks were common until the 1950s, although not in Waddon after the 1920s. (Lens of Sutton)

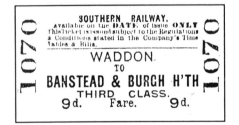

→

22. Looking towards West Croydon, we see the little used dock siding (centre) and the busy goods yard (left). The two original sidings here were increased to four and part of the yard was used by the Waddon Concrete & Building Material Co. from 1921 to 1937 for block making. This wooden footbridge was replaced by a concrete one in 1930. It was superseded by an all steel structure in 1937. (Lens of Sutton)

21. The station was opened in February 1863, sixteen years after the line. Of a later date is the signal box which remained in use until 25th November 1972. A footbridge was added in the mid-1880s. (Lens of Sutton)

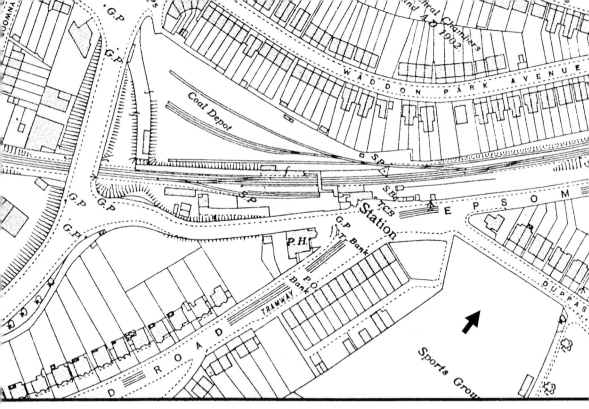

On the left of this 1933 map is the wide road bridge for Purley Way, a new road constructed in 1925 as a bypass for Croydon. It replaced a narrow bridge, the approaches of which are marked to the left of the coal depot.

23. An entirely new structure was built by the SR in 1936-37 to serve London's principal airport, which was situated one mile to the south. This was used by the RAF during WWII, service personnel generating additional rail traffic at that time. (Lens of Sutton)

24. A loading gauge stands functionless where track once led to the goods yard, which closed on 7th October 1968. The box had been resited in about 1930, prior to the rebuilding. (J.Scrace)

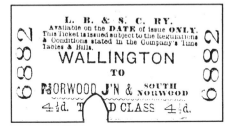

L. B. & S. C. RY.

Available on the DATE of issue ONLY.
This Ticket is issued subject to the Regulations & Conditions stated in the Company's Time Tables & Bills.

WALLINGTON

TO

NORWOOD J'N & SOUTH NORWOOD

4½d. THIRD CLASS 4½d.

6882   6882

25. Waddon might be described as SR architecture at its plainest. Seen in 1991, the booking office was then fully staffed. During WWI, a siding was laid on the down side into an aircraft factory situated about midway between Waddon and Wallington. Goods trains ceased to call there in April 1925. (J.Scrace)

BANDON HALT

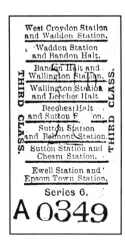

26. In an attempt to reduce the impact of competition from the trams, the LBSCR introduced motor trains of this type and opened two intermediate halts on the route. Bandon Halt was brought into use on 11th June 1906; trams from Croydon to Wallington followed on 10th November of that year. The halt closed on 7th June 1914. (Lens of Sutton)

WALLINGTON

27. Opened with the line, the station was known as "Carshalton" until 1st September 1868, when a station was provided closer to the village on the line south from Mitcham Junction. Note the hand worked points and wide foot crossing used by passengers until a subway was provided. (Lens of Sutton)

The 1882 survey confirms the rural situation of the station and the minimal facilities provided.

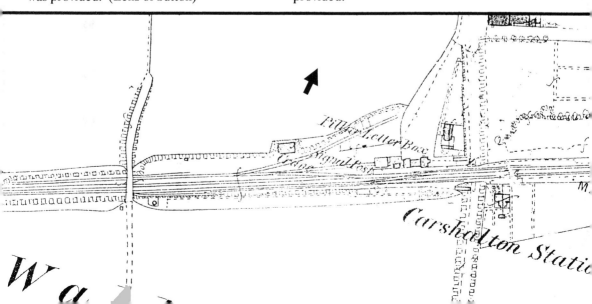

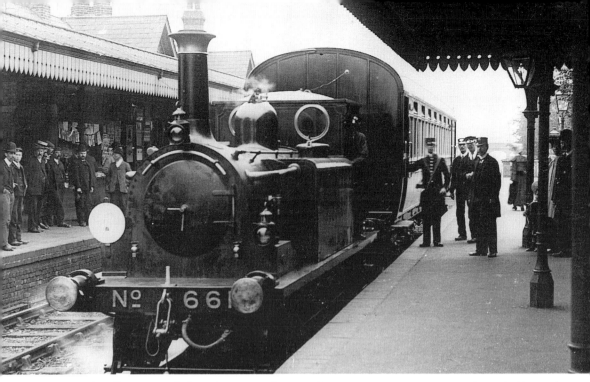

28. The first run of the West Croydon - Belmont motor train was recorded on 11th June 1906. Push - pull working was practised and tickets were issued at halts by the guard (nearest the coach and wearing a bell punch machine). This is probably the same "Terrier" as appears in picture 26. (J.R.W.Kirkby coll.)

29. The wooden part of the up platform marks the position of the bridge over Westcott Road. The lofty signals in the distance were to overcome sighting problems the platform canopy caused. (Lens of Sutton)

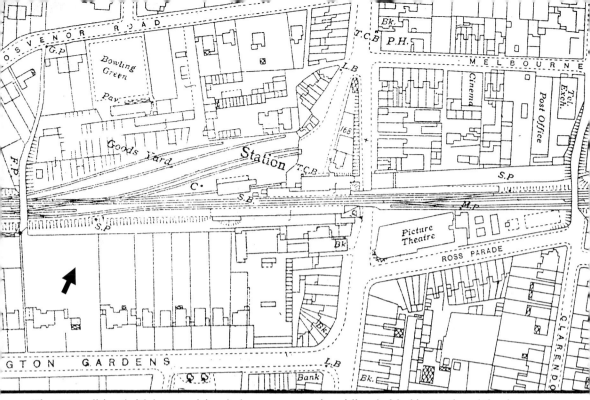

The 1913 edition (with later revisions) shows part of a 440yd long refuge siding (right), which was later fitted with a conductor rail. Top to bottom on the left is the headshunt, up line, reversing siding (added in 1916) and the down line. "C" marks the position of the crane of 5-ton capacity.

30. An Austin 7 from the mid-1920s stands close to the fire alarm pillar, a feature of the approach to many suburban stations. The station was extensively rebuilt in about 1932. (Lens of Sutton)

31. This substantial goods shed replaced the timber affair seen in picture no. 27. This signal box can also be compared with its predecessor in the same illustration. The hump in the up platform is where the gradient changes from 1 in 100 up to 1 in 143 down. The box closed on 26th November 1972. (Lens of Sutton)

32. No. 5441, a 4EPB unit, forms a London Bridge service on 6th January 1984 and, to the left of it, we can see the site of the reversing siding. A car park occupies the site of the goods yard, which closed on 6th May 1963. (F.Hornby)

L. B. & S. C. RY.
Available on the DATE of issue ONLY.
This Ticket is issued subject to the Regulations
& Conditions stated in the Company's Time
Tables and Bills.

0639
WALLINGTON
0639
Series 12)   TO   [Series 12
Sutton. su
2d.   D CLASS.   2d.

33. The station was completely redeveloped and formally reopened on 13th September 1983. The cost was £2.75m. Between 1899 and 1925 an intermediate signal box was provided between here and Sutton, but it was manned only on Epsom Race days. The down side canopy was extended in 1989. (F.Hornby)

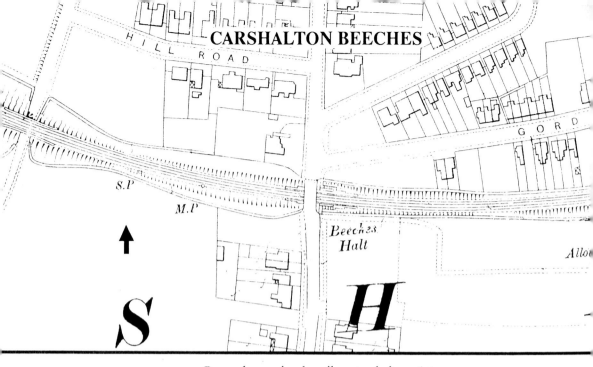

Opened as a simple rail motor halt on 1st October 1906 named "Beeches Halt", the name was changed on 1st April 1925, the day on which electric services started. This is the 1912 edition.

34. The halt was rebuilt with concrete platform components and is seen on 31st March 1925 during a railway officers' inspection. The AC electric train has a power car with a bow collector in the centre. It was fitted with driving controls which enabled it to work with two or four coaches. (Lens of Sutton)

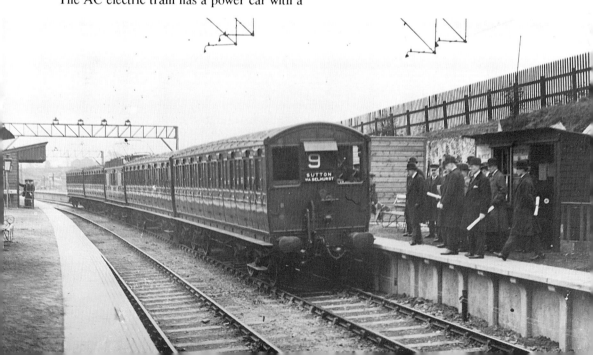

35. The simple halt shelters (left in the previous picture) were removed and this substantial station was built during 1925. Although the railway was electrified, station lighting was by gas as the railway had a contract for its supply. The footbridge was added in 1929.
(Lens of Sutton)

The 1934 edition shows that housing development in the area was complete and also reveals the increase in length of the platforms.

36. At the west end of the station Woodman-sterne Road passes over the platforms. The map shows that the bridge restricted the road width. This illustration shows widening in progress in the 1930s. An avenue of beeches lined this road, recorded for posterity in the station name. (Lens of Sutton)

S. 12.] L. B. & S. C. RY. [S. 12.
Available on the **DATE** of issue **ONLY**.
SEE CONDITIONS ON BACK.
MOTOR CAR SERVICE.
SUTTON STATION TO
BEECHES HALT
1d. THIRD CLASS. 1d.

9129 9129

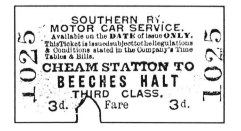

SOUTHERN RY.
MOTOR CAR SERVICE.
Available on the **DATE** of issue **ONLY**.
This Ticket is issued subject to the Regulations
& Conditions stated in the Company's Time
Tables & Bills.
CHEAM STATION TO
BEECHES HALT
THIRD CLASS.
3d. Fare 3d.

1025 1025

38. The 10.20 Guildford to Luton speeds through on 9th May 1991, the entire station being a good example of early SR architecture. Flat roofs and steel canopies were a later standard. A signal box was provided briefly, from 29th March 1925 until 30th September 1930, when it was moved to Ashtead. (J.Scrace)

37. The 1925 buildings were still in use when recorded in 1991. Passenger traffic increased tenfold in the seven years to 1932, there being 700 season tickets issued monthly by that time. The nearby Queen Mary's Hospital for Children generated considerable traffic. (J.Scrace)

SUTTON

This 1867 survey at 6" to 1 mile was undertaken just prior to the completion of the line to Mitcham Junction in 1868 - hence the missing track top right and near Sutton. Lower right is the West Croydon line and Carshalton station, now Wallington. Left is the line to Epsom with the Epsom Downs branch lower left. The new Carshalton station was built on the unfenced land near the Methodist Church. Carshalton Beeches was eventually sited above the F of Carshalton Fields.

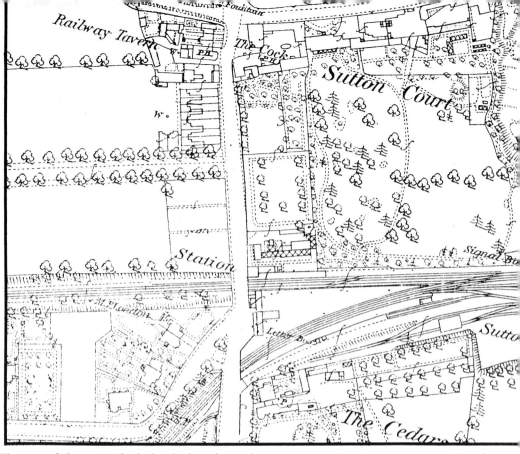

The map of about 1867 includes the junction of the Epsom Downs branch which was laid out on the site of the first station. Its wooden building was removed and served as a pavilion for Sutton Cricket Club.

The second station was built in the fork of the junction of the Epsom Downs branch. The bridge over the branch is on the left of this drawing. The entrance was at road level, passengers descending stairs outside the building to the platforms and waiting rooms.

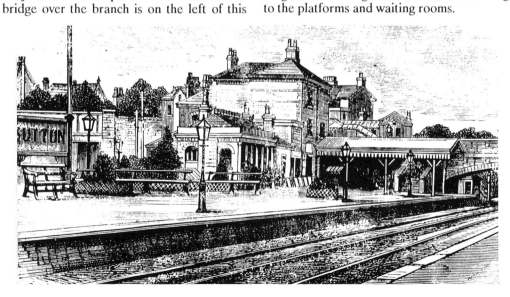

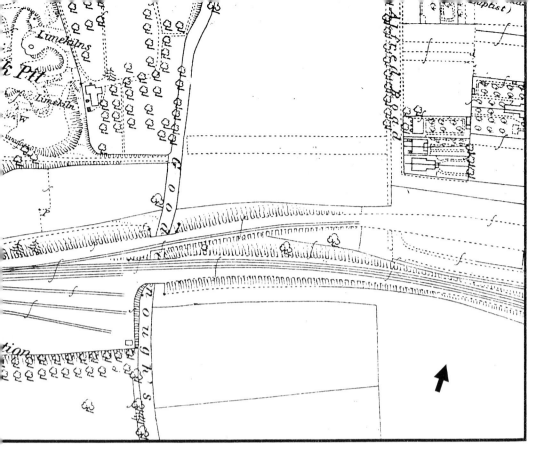

39. The buildings of the second station can be seen to the left of the signal post, as new canopies near completion. They were erected as a prelude to the building of the new offices shown in the next picture. (Lens of Sutton)

40. The third station buildings were completed in 1882 and were built above the main line tracks. Their predecessor can be seen on the right, being retained for several decades, probably for use as staff accommodation. (Lens of Sutton)

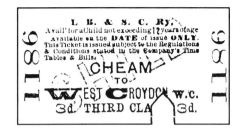

42. Class B2X no. B205 arrives with an up express on 13th April 1925 when there were still sidings each side of the main line west of the station. The quadruple track to Cheam commences just beyond the road bridge, hence the two down starting signals. (H.C.Casserley)

41. West of the station, two berthing sidings were provided off the up line and are seen in about 1890. In 1930 this became the site of the junction for the new St.Helier line, when the end of the up double track was moved further west. The two down tracks of the quadruple section to Cheam remained unchanged. (J.R.W.Kirkby coll.)

43. A Sunday stopping train from London Bridge to Brighton via Horsham and Steyning passes over the junction, hauled by class B1 0-4-2 no. B176. All four platform lines had overhead gantries in the late 1920s but only platforms 3 and 4 were wired. (J.R.W.Kirkby coll.)

44. A complete rebuild of all the street level premises resulted in this neat and functional structure in 1928. Sutton's population had grown from 1400 to 14000 in the first 40 years of the railway and was still increasing. (Lens of Sutton)

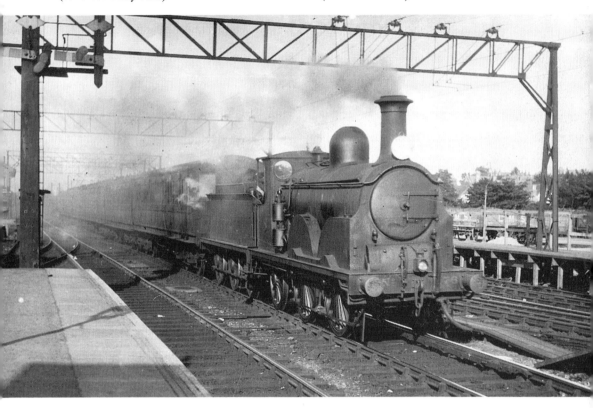

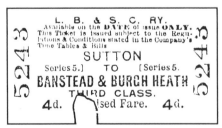

45. Coal for domestic use and for the residential institutions was the main commodity handled by freight services on the Epsom Downs line. Class E4 0-6-2T no.2504 squeals round the 12 chain radius curve on 31st March 1936 before starting the climb to Belmont. (H.F.Wheeller)

46. Running into platform 3 in August 1949 is 4SUB no. S4324, the third coach being a recent all steel addition to the set. An eight-lever box was provided here in 1878 but this box dates from 1916 and has twelve levers. The two arms marked "S" allowed trains to shunt over the crossover seen in the next picture. (D.Clayton)

47. During the 1950s the shunt arms were removed, the box ceasing to function on 30th July 1969 when colour lights came into use. The AC overhead wiring had extended (on the down) one train length beyond the crossover, to enable trains to move from platforms 4 to 3. (J.R.W.Kirkby)

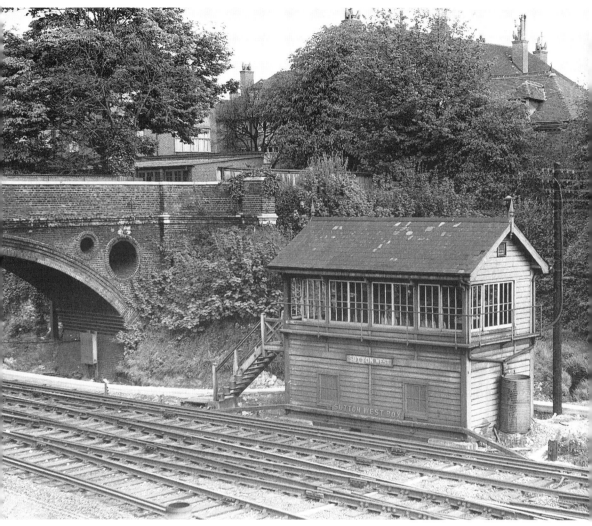

48. Sutton West box was west of Bridge Road bridge on the down side, and controlled the junction with the St.Helier line from its opening on 5th January 1930 until 17th July 1955. The weight reducing bridge design can be seen elsewhere on this route. This box also controlled the quadruple track to (and including) Cheam. It had been built in 1899 to ease the work of Sutton Junction Box and was initially named Sutton Main Line. (J.J.Smith)

SOUTHERN RAILWAY.
This ticket is issued subject to the Company's Bye-laws, Regulations and Conditions in their Time Tables, Notices and Book of Regulations.
Available on DAY of issue ONLY.

Carshalton Beeches to

Carshalton Beeches   Carshalton Beeches
Sutton   Sutton

SUTTON

THIRD CLASS   (S-17)   THIRD CLASS
Fare 1½d.   Fare 1½d.

5662   5662

2nd - SINGLE   SINGLE - 2nd

Carshalton Beeches to
Carshalton Beeches   Carshalton Beeches
Mitcham Junction,   Mitcham Junction,
Morden South or   Morden South or
South Merton   South Merton
MITCHAM JUNCTION, MORDEN SOUTH
or SOUTH MERTON
via Sutton
(S)   1/6 Fare 1/6   (S)
For conditions see over   For conditions see over

2200   2200

49. An Epsom to Norwood Junction freight has just passed over Sutton West Junction and enters platform 1 in 1957. The locomotive is class E2 0-6-0T no.32104 from 1914. The down main starting signal is silhouetted against a hole in the road bridge, the building on the right housing the postal sorting office. (J.R.W.Kirkby coll.)

50. Each platform had two starting signals, one for the West Croydon line and one for the Mitcham Junction route. Platform 1 (right) had been greatly widened in 1882 but much excavation was required owing to it being partly in cutting. The canopy on platform 3 has been rebuilt but otherwise the structures remained little altered in 1992. There had once been a bay platform on the right. (D.Cullum coll.)

51. Track alterations in 1925 allowed the arrival and/or departure of trains simultaneously on the Mitcham Junction-Epsom and West Croydon-Epsom Downs routes. This was achieved by creating four parallel tracks in front of Sutton Junction Box (left), which was in use from 4th January 1925 until 3rd October 1982. On the left is a train from the Mid-Sussex line, while on the right is the goods yard which closed on 7th October 1968, two years after this photograph was taken. One engineer's siding remained in 1992. (J.N.Faulkner)

52. From 26th November 1981 until 4th November 1982 there were no through trains onto the branch, for reasons explained later. Operating the shuttle service on 15th September 1982 is the preserved 4SUB unit, which had been restored to its original green livery, except at its outer ends. (J.Scrace)

53. Working the 09.35 Epsom Downs to Victoria service through platform 3 on 1st May 1990 is class 455 no.5825, a type introduced in 1982. With the full use of colour light signalling at Sutton that year it was still possible to start up trains from any of the four platforms. (J.Scrace)

L. B. & S. C. RY.
Available on the **DATE** of issue **ONLY**.
This Ticket is issued subject to the Regulations
& Conditions stated in the Company's Time
Tables & Bills.
SUTTON
Series 8]   **TO**   [Series 8
BELMONT be
1d. **THIRD CLASS.** 1d.

4928   4928

54. Although the number of through travel opportunities southwards from Sutton has reduced over the years, the northern destinations increased considerably in May 1990, when Thameslink trains started to serve the town. This is the 11.00 Luton to Guildford service on 12th February 1992. (M.Turvey)

55. Viewed from Bridge Road on 9th April 1985 is the 09.21 Dorking to Victoria service at Sutton West Junction. The class 415 units (4EPB) were soon to be replaced by 455s. Behind the train the line to St.Helier and Wimbledon drops away at 1 in 44. (D.Brown)

Sutton is featured with photographs and an 1896 map in our *Mitcham Junction Lines* album.

56. No rail tour including Sutton would be complete without a visit to Lens of Sutton. Lens refers to part of a camera and not the proprietor, Mr.J.L.Smith, seen here amongst the unbelievable range of transport photographs, books and magazines. Back numbers of the latter are a speciality. (A.C.Mott)

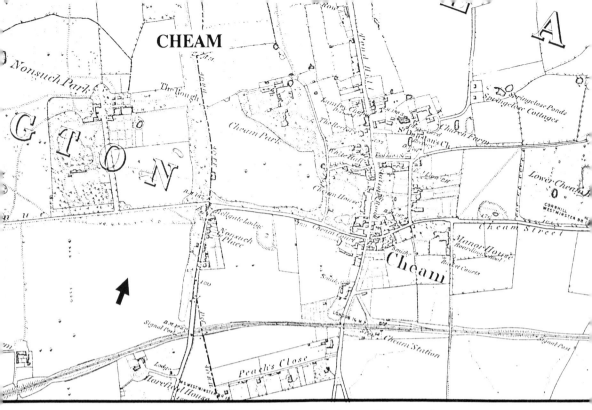

CHEAM

The 6" to 1 mile reveals the small extent of
the village and its proximity to the station,
which opened with the line on 10th May 1847.

57. Looking west from Hale's Bridge, it is
evident that the sidings were, at one time, more
curved than shown on the 1913 map. The land
on the left was the site of the later goods yard
and station approach. (J.R.W.Kirkby coll.)

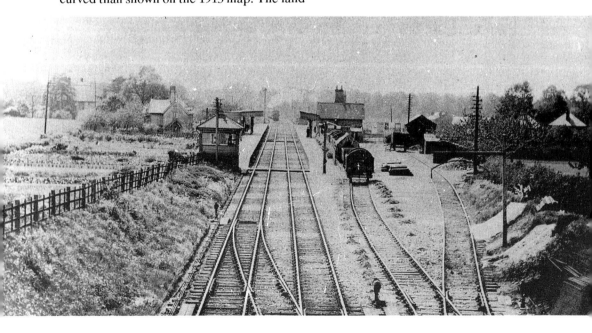

58. An eastward view shows Hale's Bridge
before it was rebuilt to accommodate quadruple track and new sidings in 1911. The
tapered wooden signal post was a typical
LBSCR feature. (J.R.W.Kirkby coll.)

The 1913 edition confirms that two short
sidings still sufficed for local traffic.

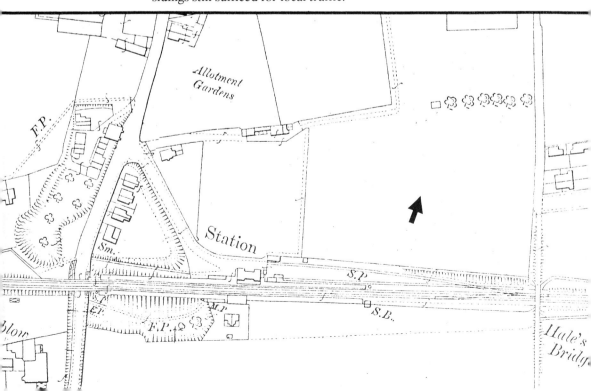

59. Associated with the quadrupling was the complete rebuilding of the station, the new offices being on the down side (right) instead of the up, as previously. Plans were made for an island platform and the subway skylights positioned accordingly. Express trains were to call at the island enabling passengers to transfer to or from AC electric trains which would terminate here, using the outer platforms. Note that the single brick arch was replaced by a very long steel bridge and that the down fast line was on the site of the proposed island. (Lens of Sutton)

The 1934 edition at 20" to 1 mile has quadruple track and a headshunt on the right. The two extra tracks from Sutton West Junction came into use on 1st October 1911 and enabled expresses (on the inner pair of tracks) to overtake local trains. The enlarged goods yard was in use until 28th September 1964.

L. B. & S. C. RY.
Available on the DATE of issue ONLY.
This Ticket is issued subject to the Regulations
& Conditions stated in the Company's Time
Tables & Bills.
CROYDON WEST
TO
CHEAM c
5½d. THIRD CLASS. 5½d.

7096   7096

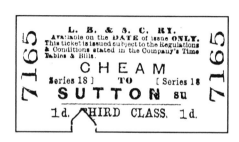

L. B. & S. C. RY.
Available on the DATE of issue ONLY.
This ticket is issued subject to the Regulations
& Conditions stated in the Company's Time
Tables & Bills.
CHEAM
Series 18]   TO   [Series 18
SUTTON su
1d. THIRD CLASS. 1d.

7165   7165

60. A class D1 0-4-2T is entering the up platform with two halves of two divisible suburban train sets. Owing to the advent of WWI the overhead wires did not reach Cheam. As already seen, they came to Sutton in 1925, by which time complete electrification of the route with conductor rail had been agreed, and the grand scheme for Cheam did not materialise. (J.R.W.Kirkby coll.)

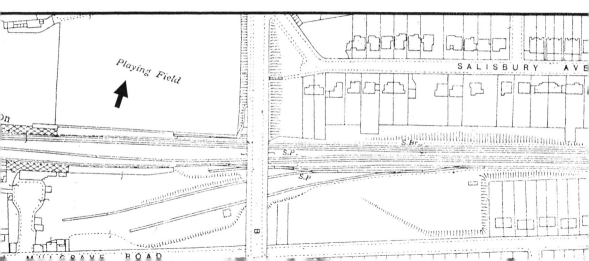

61. Looking east, Cheam station is in the distance, and the sidings for terminating suburban trains are evident. Two trains were berthed here overnight from 1911, but as only one engine could be released, the other train had to be propelled in. This would have been the limit of the wires had electrification been completed as first planned. (D.Cullum coll.)

62. Third rail electric services commenced on 3rd March 1929, but only the local lines were electrified. A Portsmouth express speeds through, hauled by class B4 no.B65. The fast lines received conductor rails prior to the electrification of main line services in 1938. (J.R.W.Kirkby coll.)

63. Class C no.31229 is working a Christmas parcels special on 24th December 1955 and is bound for Dorking North. The vans had been detached from a Bricklayers Arms to Brighton train at New Cross Gate. The concrete bridge was built in about 1927 to accommodate the Sutton bypass. The steel one remained alongside before being dismantled and reused in 1935 to form the present Guildford station footbridge. (J.J.Smith)

64. This signal box was in use from 1st October 1911 until 28th May 1978 and is seen on 14th April 1968. It was built on a substantial brick arch and was situated at the west end of the up platform - see picture 60 and the 1934 map. The box was destroyed by an arsonist on 14th January 1983 while the Bluebell Railway was negotiating its purchase. (J.Scrace)

66. In the early 1950s, the quadruple track was largely eliminated, except within the station limits, but the berthing sidings had been removed earlier. The through lines were removed in 1977-78, leaving this vast gap between the platforms as a memorial to unfulfilled dreams. The train is the 14.50 Dorking to Victoria on 9th March 1992. (J.Scrace)

65. The south elevation showed bold functional Edwardian styling. The local population
had trebled to a mere 3400 in the first 50 years
of the community but grew rapidly thereafter.
(C.Hall)

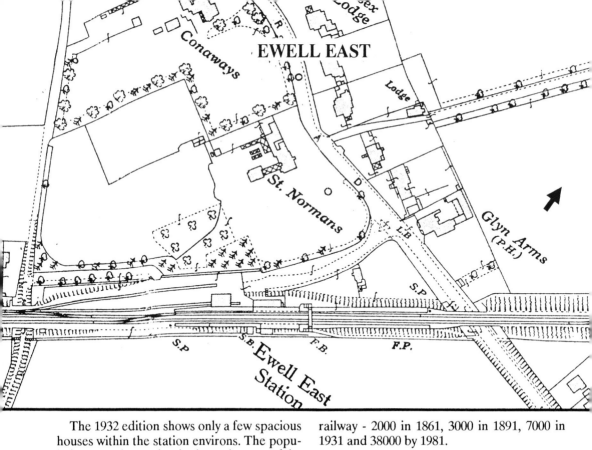

EWELL EAST

The 1932 edition shows only a few spacious houses within the station environs. The population growth was slow in the early years of the railway - 2000 in 1861, 3000 in 1891, 7000 in 1931 and 38000 by 1981.

67. The station opened with the line, but the suffix "East" was not applied until 9th July 1923, despite the LSWR's station on the other side of the village having been in use since 1859. Class C2X 0-6-0 no.32546 is passing through the down platform with the gauging coach, known to some as the "Porcupine". (Lens of Sutton)

68. The pronunciation of Ewell is "you-all". The goods yard was in use until 4th April 1960 and the signal box until 11th May 1969. The wicket gate on the left was later enclosed by the awning seen in the previous photograph. (D.Cullum coll.)

69. Unit no.5428 brakes on the falling gradient of 1 in 100, while working the 16.25 Victoria-Horsham on 14th May 1991. Such gradients for stations were frowned upon during the later years of railway construction. The footbridge and canopies date from about 1890. (J.Scrace)

70. Seen in 1991, the main building appears to date from 1847, although the pebble-dash gives a more modern appearance. As at Cheam, the booking office was staffed in the mornings only, although for fewer hours. (J.Scrace)

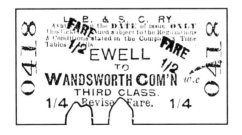

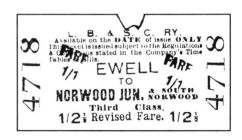

SOUTH OF EWELL EAST

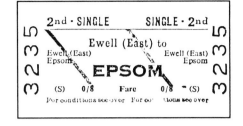

71. Seen from Windmill Lane Bridge in June 1956 is class 4 2-6-4T no.80084 with assorted horse boxes, bound for Epsom in connection with horse sales. Each vehicle had a compartment for a groom. (D.Clayton)

EPSOM TOWN

The 1888 map includes the bridge for
Church Road, four wagon turntables and a 40ft
locomotive turntable.

72. The LBSCR established its terminus to the east of the town, which had already gained fame on account of the "bowel purging" medicinal salts (magnesium sulphate) discovered in a spring near Ashtead in the 17th century. It became a through station in 1859 when services were extended to Leatherhead.
(Lens of Sutton)

73. The two-road engine shed housed locomotives overnight and probably a stand-by engine during the day. Class D1 0-4-2T no.607 may have been "spare" when recorded in the early 1900s. (R.C.Riley coll.)

74. Photographed on 24th May 1926 is class D1 no.B612. The shed closed after completion of electrification in 1929, when D1s were largely retired to rural routes. (H.C.Casserley)

75. An up train passes the locomotive depot on 18th March 1928, class B1 no. B174 being admired by a railwayman in the ashpit. The suburban train in the loop will probably shunt back into the station before leaving for London. (H.C.Casserley)

SOUTHERN RY.
Available on DAY of issue ONLY.
This ticket is issued subject to the By-laws, Regulations and Conditions stated in the Company's Time Tables, Bills and Notices.
EPSOM TOWN
TO
CHICHESTER ch
THIRD CLASS.
6/6   Fare   6/6
2748

SOUTHERN
Available on the DATE of issue ONLY.
This ticket is issued subject to the Regulations & Conditions stated in the Company's Time Tables & Bills.
EPSOM TOWN
TO
LONDON
THIRD CLASS.
1/6   Fare   1/6
6163

L. B. & S. C. RY.
Available on the Date of issue ONLY.
This Ticket is issued subject to the Regulations & Conditions stated in the Company's Time Tables & Bills.
EPSOM TOWN
TO
DORKING d
7½d. THIRD CLASS. 7½d.
1831

L. B. & S. C. Ry.
Available on the Date of issue ONLY.
This Ticket is issued subject to the Regulations & Conditions stated in the Company's Time Tables & Bills.
EPSOM TOWN
TO
CHEAM c
2½d. THIRD CLASS. 2½d.
7059

76. A horse box stands at the dock as class B1 no.B181 arrives with an up train in dismal weather on 10th February 1929, the conductor rails now being in place. The station was busy on race days as the town was well provided with pubs. To travel on the branch was to remain sober. (H.C.Casserley)

77. The same train stands in the up platform and we have the opportunity to note the position of the subway steps, the up starting signal for the down platform and the signal box. The down side offices were still standing in 1992. (H.C.Casserley)

78. The passenger platforms were closed with the advent of electric services on 3rd March 1929 and the former locomotive depot site was fenced off for use by Longhurst & Son for building materials. They had the use of two sidings and Stone & Co. had a siding into Nonsuch Brickworks. (Lens of Sutton)

80. The signal box was renamed "East Goods" on 7th July 1931 and closed on 3rd October 1967. Class U1 no.31899 heads an up goods on 4th August 1962 and passes the yard, which closed on 3rd May 1965. It had a 5 ton crane east of the goods shed. (A.N.Davenport)

79. Goods traffic continued to be handled at Town station, the new station only dealing with passengers and parcels. The suffix "Town" was in use in the 1870s and again from July 1923. Standing by the dock on 28th November 1948 are class E4 no.2476 and class E6X no.2411. (A.N.Davenport)

EPSOM

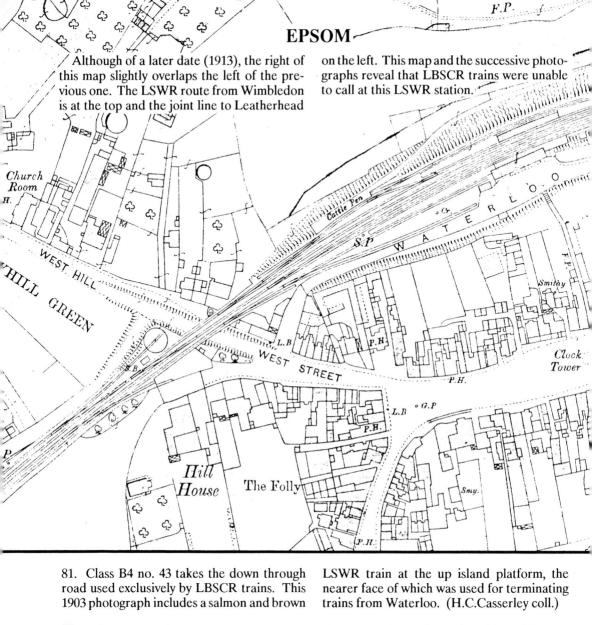

Although of a later date (1913), the right of this map slightly overlaps the left of the previous one. The LSWR route from Wimbledon is at the top and the joint line to Leatherhead is at the bottom on the left. This map and the successive photographs reveal that LBSCR trains were unable to call at this LSWR station.

81. Class B4 no. 43 takes the down through road used exclusively by LBSCR trains. This 1903 photograph includes a salmon and brown LSWR train at the up island platform, the nearer face of which was used for terminating trains from Waterloo. (H.C.Casserley coll.)

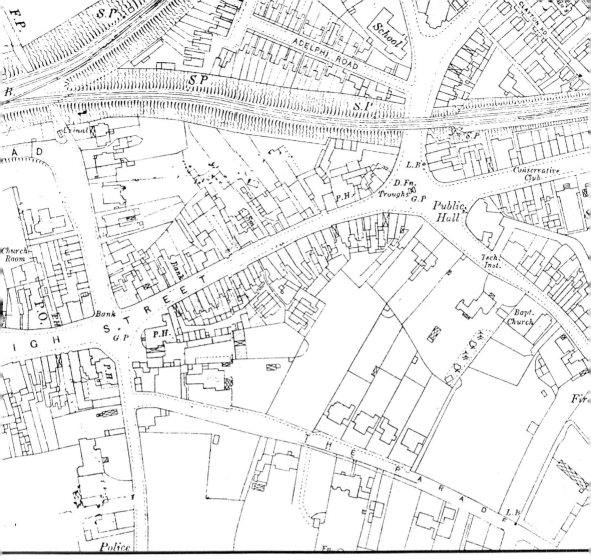

82. Ex-LBSCR class I3 no. 78 is on the up through line on 2nd October 1926, bound for Sutton. The conductor rail had been used by trains from Waterloo since 12th July 1925. Goods facilities were withdrawn from this station on 2nd January 1928. (H.C.Casserley)

83. In the summer of 1928 the SR started work on a scheme to end the nonsense of having two stations in the town. This photograph was taken from a temporary footbridge on 10th February 1929, the line from Sutton being on the right. (H.C.Casserley)

84. The first new platform to be built was no. 1 (left), this being created on a newly raised embankment. A temporary timber platform was erected over the down local line while platform 4 was constructed. No. 3 was built later, on the site of the temporary one. This and the next three pictures were taken soon after the completion of the work. (Railway Engineer)

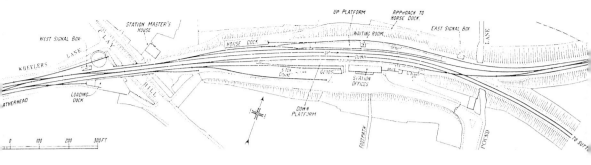

Plan of the station prior to the alterations in 1928-29.

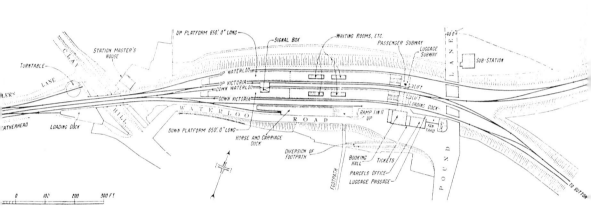

Plan of the station after the completion of alterations in 1929.

Plan of the new offices.

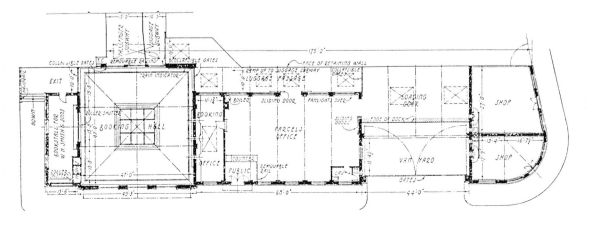

85. The station approach and buildings were reconstructed; the booking hall linking directly to a new subway. The towers for the luggage lifts are evident. Off the right of the picture, the brick arch over Pound Lane was replaced with three separate steel girder bridges. (Railway Engineer)

2427 | 2nd - SINGLE   SINGLE - 2nd | 2427

| 2nd - SINGLE | SINGLE - 2nd |
| Wallington to |
| Wallington | Wallington |
| Banstead or Ewell E. | Banstead or Ewell E. |
| BANSTEAD or EWELL EAST |
| (S)   10d.   FARE   10d.   (S) |
| For condit'ns see over   For condit'ns see over |

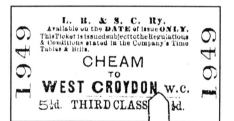

L. B. & S. C. Ry.
Available on the **DATE** of issue **ONLY.**
This Ticket is issued subject to the Regulations & Conditions stated in the Company's Time Tables & Bills.
1949   **CHEAM**   1949
TO
WEST CROYDON w.c.
5½d. THIRD CLASS ½d.

86. This is the view from the new signal box, which replaced East Box and West Box on 24th February 1929. The steel faced canopy is glazed each side and roofed with zinc on boards in the centre. The headcode indicates Waterloo to Effingham Junction. (Railway Engineer)

87. A berthing siding was provided each side of the Leatherhead line - hence the ringed signals in picture 84. In pre-electric days a turntable was also available - see map. The headcode V was for Victoria via Mitcham Junction. (Railway Engineer)

88. Sixty levers were installed, of which only six were spare. The box closed on 29th July 1990 but since 11th May 1969 it had been controlling colour lights, apart from two ground signals. Otherwise the station was largely in its 1929 condition as the 17.12 Waterloo to Dorking departed on 14th May 1991. The box received a listed building status. (J.Scrace)

Other views of this station can be found in our *Epsom to Horsham* album.

Epsom Downs Branch

89. We start our visit to the branch by looking at two special race day features. Three intermediate signal boxes were in use from 1902 to 1955 on race days only but their signal spectacles were unglazed and not provided with lamps, as they were not used during darkness. However the distant arms near Ventnor Road Bridge, Sutton, were in regular use and can be seen to be fully equipped. The boxes were designated A, B and C and the arms were normally removed for most of the year.
(D.Clayton)

90. The other notable feature of the branch was the working of Pullman trains for Epsom Races. For many years Lord Derby hired one such train for his friends. Class E5 0-6-2T no. 2404 pilots H class 0-4-4T no. 1548 on Derby Day 1935. The train is the 12.35pm from Victoria and is seen south of Belmont. The two pole routes suggest that one is SR and the other is GPO. (Dr.I.C.Allen)

BELMONT

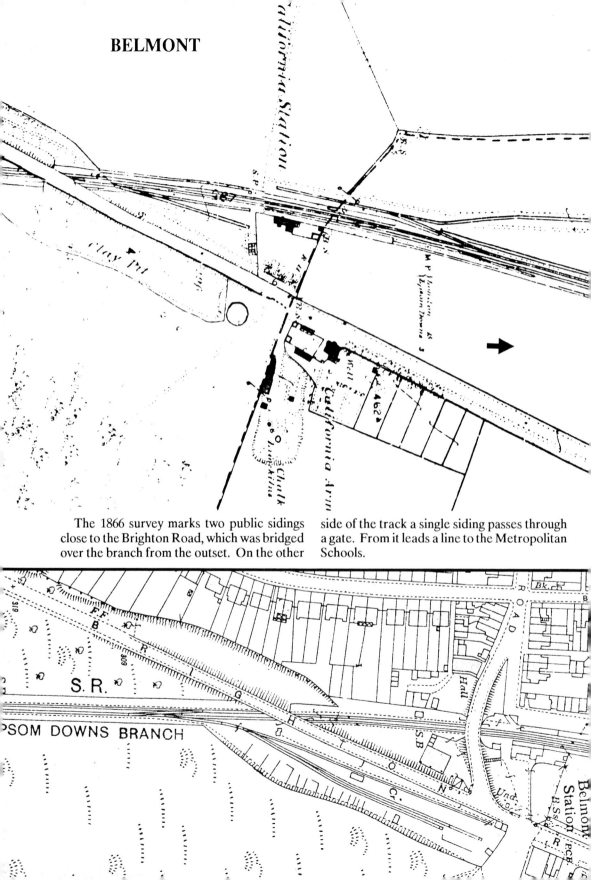

The 1866 survey marks two public sidings close to the Brighton Road, which was bridged over the branch from the outset. On the other side of the track a single siding passes through a gate. From it leads a line to the Metropolitan Schools.

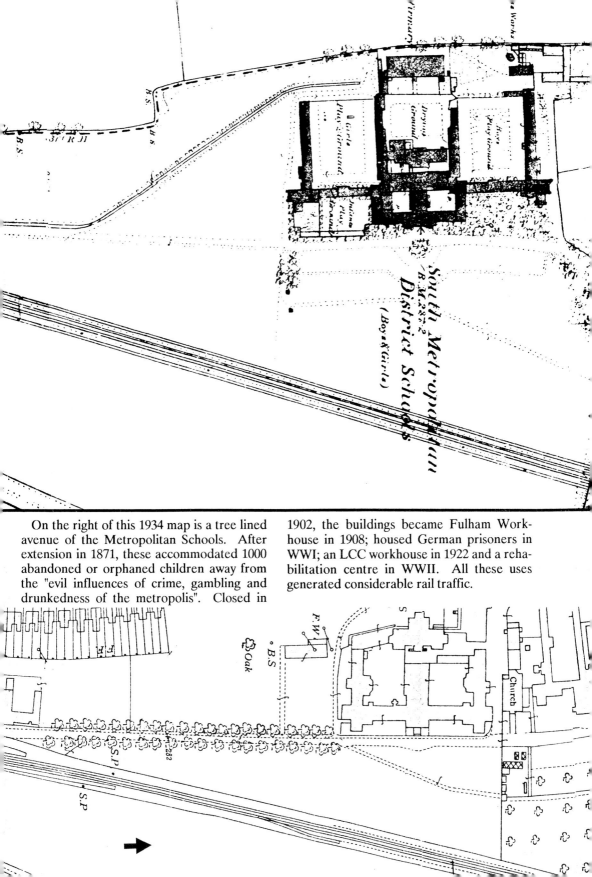

On the right of this 1934 map is a tree lined avenue of the Metropolitan Schools. After extension in 1871, these accommodated 1000 abandoned or orphaned children away from the "evil influences of crime, gambling and drunkedness of the metropolis". Closed in 1902, the buildings became Fulham Workhouse in 1908; housed German prisoners in WWI; an LCC workhouse in 1922 and a rehabilitation centre in WWII. All these uses generated considerable rail traffic.

91. The station opened with the line on 22nd May 1865 and was named "California" after a nearby inn. Owing to a risk of inward parcels being exported, the name was changed on 1st October 1875. The LBSCR delivery van and station master's house are evident. (J.R.W.Kirkby coll.)

92. A northward view from the road bridge includes a siding (lower left), used by the Metropolitan Schools until about 1889, and a rail motor, worked by class D1 0-4-2T no. 259. It will have run past the refuge siding on the right, propelled over the crossover and is entering the up platform as the fireman removes the headcode disc. (Lens of Sutton)

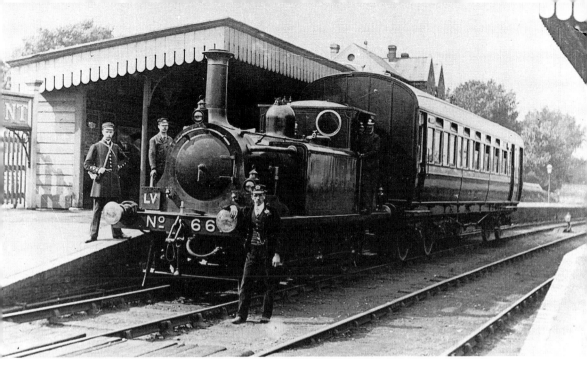

93. Most of the motor trains introduced in 1906 operated between West Croydon and Belmont only. This appears to be Terrier no. 661, formerly *Sutton*. The conductor/guard is standing close to the "Last Vehicle" board, prior to departing north. (Lens of Sutton)

94. A bridge replaced the level crossing at the end of the platforms in 1884 but this is its successor, built by the Surrey County Council. This photograph was taken from the Brighton Road bridge on 18th April 1939, as class I3 no. 2091 was passing with a race special. The land on the right was the site of the earlier goods yard, shown on the 1866 map. (J.R.W.Kirkby)

95. The goods yard was moved south of the Brighton Road in 1889 and remained in use until 6th January 1969, although only handling coal in its final three years. This glimpse from a passing train dates from 1936. (H.F.Wheeller)

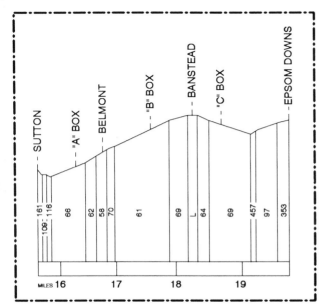

97. New offices of CLASP construction were completed on the down side in May 1970, shelters being provided on the up side. Singling of the branch took place on 3rd October 1982 - this is the northward view shortly after. (J.Scrace)

96. The signal box was in use until 21st December 1969, having been built in 1909. The footbridge was erected in 1928, having previously served at Folkestone Junction. The down side buildings were destroyed by enemy action on 11th October 1940 and were replaced by a simple brick shelter. The up side timber-built offices were erected in 1938 and contained sufficient office accommodation.
(Lens of Sutton)

BANSTEAD

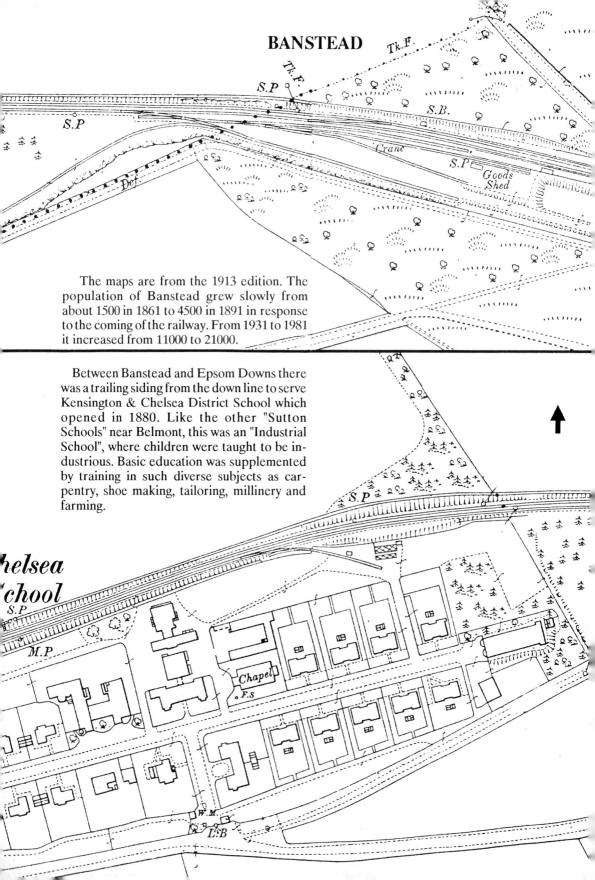

The maps are from the 1913 edition. The population of Banstead grew slowly from about 1500 in 1861 to 4500 in 1891 in response to the coming of the railway. From 1931 to 1981 it increased from 11000 to 21000.

Between Banstead and Epsom Downs there was a trailing siding from the down line to serve Kensington & Chelsea District School which opened in 1880. Like the other "Sutton Schools" near Belmont, this was an "Industrial School", where children were taught to be industrious. Basic education was supplemented by training in such diverse subjects as carpentry, shoe making, tailoring, millinery and farming.

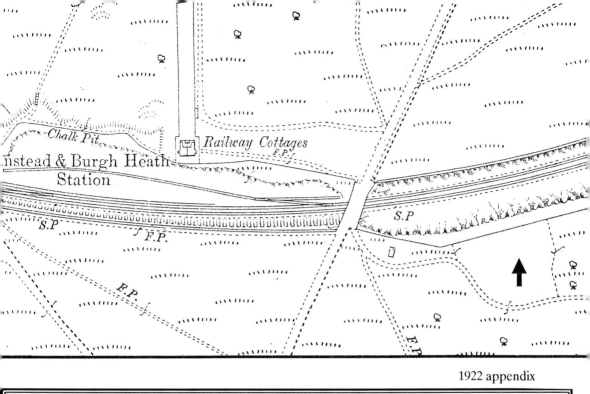

Chalk Pit
Railway Cottages
F.P.
nstead & Burgh Heath Station
S.P.
F.P.
S.P.
F.P.
F.P.
F.P.

Banstead: Kensington and Chelsea District School Siding.—This Siding is used for Goods Traffic to and from the Kensington and Chelsea District Schools, and joins the Down Line about 400 yards South of Banstead Station. The Points leading to and from the Siding are fitted with Annett's key, which also locks the Down Signals at Banstead Station. The Down Signals at Banstead cannot be lowered unless the key is in the lock in the Signal Box, nor can the Points at the Siding be opened unless the key is in the lock at the Points. The Station Master at Banstead must instruct the Driver and Guards when to call at the Siding and send a Porter to bring back the key.

98. The station opened with the line and had the suffix "& Burgh Heath" from 1898 until 1928. The stationmaster's house is on the left, the station offices being suitably annotated. This was for the benefit of passing aviators searching for Croydon Airport. Passengers stride towards the entrance in June 1936. (H.F.Wheeller)

99. Standing in the up platform on 23rd April 1935 are two 3SUBs separated by two trailer coaches, a standard formation in peak hours. The shunting engine is class E3 0-6-2T no.2169. The goods yard was mainly used for coal traffic but included a crane of 4 ton 10 cwt capacity, partly visible. (H.F.Wheeller)

100. A return race special approaches the station with two class I3s, no.2085 piloting no.2029. The van would have been for the sole use of the guard who would not otherwise have had access to an emergency brake. Race goers would have had no luggage. The siding on the left ran into a chalk pit. (Dr.I.C.Allen)

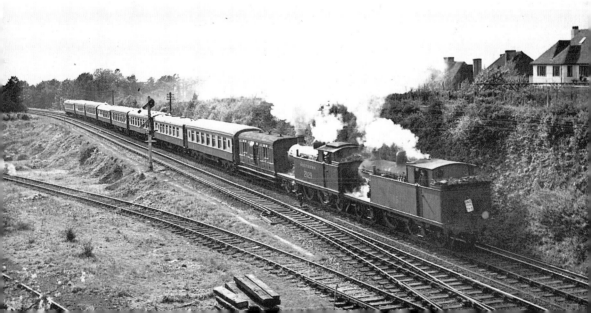

101. As the platforms were in cutting, it was convenient to build the offices on a bridge between them. The down platform (right) was lengthened at the time of electrification in 1928 (and further in 1983-84), but the other one had to wait until after WWII. The canopies were extended in 1935 but to a new profile. This is a 1962 photograph. (J.N.Faulkner)

102. Freight traffic on the branch was light but in the exceptionally severe winter of 1963-64 there was an unusual demand for coal. Class 4 4-6-0 no.75075 arrives on 14th December 1963 in freezing conditions which continued unabated for over three months, with snow lying almost continuously from 26th December. (S.C.Nash)

103. Bound for Epsom Downs with an LCGB railtour on 5th July 1964 is class 2 2-6-0 no.78038. The train of smart Bulleid coaches included a buffet in the third vehicle. The goods yard was soon to close, this being effected on 7th September 1964. (J.J.Smith)

104. The same train is returning past the 1903 signal box, which remained in use until 21st December 1969, when colour light signalling was introduced. The "Surrey Wanderer" ran from Waterloo via Twickenham, Shepperton, Kingston, Wimbledon, Mitcham, West Croydon, Epsom Downs, Tulse Hill, Crystal Palace, Beckenham Junction, East Croydon, Caterham, Purley, Tattenham Corner, Kensington Olympia to Victoria. Adults - 30 shillings. (J.J.Smith)

LONDON, SUTTON, BANSTEAD AND BURGH HEATH, and EPSOM DOWNS.—L. B. & S. C.

Up.   **Week Days.**

Miles		mrn	mrn	mrn		mrn	mrn	mrn	mrn		mrn			mrn		aft	aft	aft		aft		aft	aft
	Epsom Downs.....dep.	....	8	8	....		8	10	9 42	m	....	1050	....	....	1132	....	....	....	1233				
1¼	Banstead & Burgh Heath	7 45	8 12	8 33	....	8 58	9 14	9 46	1011	....	1054	....	m	1136	....	12 2	m	1237	....	1 12		....	26 m
3	Belmont.....[183, 184	7 47	8 15	8 35	....	9 09	9 19	9 49	1013	....	1057	1110	1120	1139	....	12 4	1236	1240	....	1 14		1 22	1 27
4	Sutton 170, 176, 181, arr	7 51	8 19	8 39	....	9 49	9 22	9 53	1017	....	11 1	1113	1132	1143	....	12 9	1239	1244	....	1 18		1 26	1 30
17½	181 London B. 183 arr.	8 41	9 59	16	....	9 41	10 5	1022	1050	....	1159	1159	....	1217	....	1312	1312	1 43		....		2 20	....
16½	170 Victoria 176.. "	8 32	8 53	9 16	....	9 30	9 55	1037	1058	....	1150	....	1235	1258	....	1258	....	1 57		1 57		2 17	....

Up.   **Week Days—Continued.**

		aft		aft		aft		aft	aft		aft	aft		aft	aft		aft		aft	aft
	Epsom Downs.........dep.							2 17	m		m	m		2 59	m		3 38		3 45	4 20
	Banstead and Burgh Heath	Sats. only	m	1 47	Except Sats.	2 0	Except Sats.	2 34	2 21	Except Sats.	2 37	2 75	Sats. only	3 37	3 0	Except Sats.	3 42	Sats. only	49 4	24
	Belmont.........[183, 184	1 40		1 49		2 4		2 24	2 36		2 40	3 0		3 39	3 4		3 49		3 56	4 31
	Sutton 170, 176, 181, arr.	1 43		1 53		2 8		2 25	2 40		2 43	3 4		3 43	3 49				4 52	5 32
	181 London Bridge 183 arr.	2 46		2 46		3 13		3 32	3 32		3 32	3 56			4 44		4 44		5 21	
	170 Victoria 176...... "			2 59		2 46		3 32	3 32		4 0			4 52		4 52		5 32		

Up.   **Week Days—Continued.**

		aft	m	aft		aft		aft	aft	aft	aft	aft		aft	aft	aft	aft
	Epsom Downs.........dep.	5 10				6 25	m		7 22	m								
	Banstead and Burgh Heath	4 52	5 14	5 40	Except Sats.	6 1	m	6 29	6 47	6 53	7 26	7 48	8 10		8 24	8 45	9 25	9 50
	Belmont.........[183, 184	4 54	5 17	5 42		6 3		6 29	6 32	6 49	6 55	7 29	7 50	8 12		8 24	8 47	9 27
	Sutton 170, 176, 181, arr.	4 58	5 21	5 46		6 7		6 36	6 36	6 53	6 59	7 33	7 54	8 16		8 27	8 51	9 31
	181 London Bridge 183 arr.	6 26	5 46	6 54		7 13		7 13	7 49		7 49	8 58	5 4		....	9 25	9 35	1012
	170 Victoria 176...... "	5 32	6 14			6 44		7 12		7 48		8 55		9 30	9 42	16	8 1127	

Up.   **Sundays.**

		mrn	mrn	mrn		aft	aft	aft		aft	aft	aft		aft	aft	aft
	Epsom Downs.........dep.	m	m		....		m			m	m			m			
	Banstead and Burgh Heath	10 7	1035	1147	....	m	2 45	3 35	....	3 55	4 37	5	5	5 43	6	5 07	55
	Belmont.........[183, 184	10 9	1039	1149	....	1252	2 48	3 37	....	3 58	4 39	5	5	5 45	6	5 27	57
	Sutton 170, 178, 182, arr.	1013	1043	1153	....	1252	2 52	3 41	....	4 24	4 35	5 13	....	5 49	6	5 68	1
	182 London Bridge 183 arr.	1110	....	....	....		3 32		....			5 54	....	6 23		3 8	45
	170 Victoria 178...... "	1117	....	1253	....		4 23		....		4 45	5 33	....		7 237	30	8 41

A Leaves London Bridge at 5 15 aft. on Saturdays.	**e** Except Saturdays.	* Over ½ mile to Tattenham Corner Station, S. E. & C.
B Leaves London Bridge at 6 16 aft. on Saturdays.	**m** Motor Car, 3rd class only.	
	s Saturdays only.	

July 1919

105. Only the down platform remained in use after the 1982 singling, the canopies being removed in favour of a glazed shelter. Class 455 no.5802 forms the 15.43 from Victoria on 14th May 1991. Note the mirror necessary for driver-only operation. (J.Scrace)

EPSOM DOWNS

106. A specially composed photograph taken from the signal box in 1907 includes the Royal Train on the extreme left. Note the earth mounds acting as stops at the ends of the engine release roads. (Lens of Sutton)

107. This post card is included as it shows the station in relation to the Downs and serves as a reminder that on non-race weekends in the summer the railway carried South Londoners for a day out in the country. This was a popular destination for Sunday school outings - there are swings in the background. (Lens of Sutton)

108. A continuation of the cover picture includes class E5 0-6-2T no.574 and the 42ft turntable on the right. This was removed in 1931, as it was little used by then. (F.Burtt/NRM)

109. The LBSCR could be seen at its smartest on race days. Note the gleaming ivory upper body panels and matching wheel rims. Class I3 no.21 was also well presented. The flag bears the words *RAILWAY STATION* for the benefit of those lost in the crowds on the Downs. (F.Burtt/NRM)

110. The Royal Train on Derby Day 1908 was hauled by class I2 no.15, the centre coach being the King's saloon, a 52ft long 12-wheeler. The LBSCR loading gauge was greater at eaves height than that of its neighbours, hence the massive guard's ducket. (E.R.Lacey coll.)

The 1913 edition shows the layout at its optimum.

112. From 1928 until 1972, electric stock was berthed here overnight and interior cleaning was carried out, as witnessed on 4th June 1949. By that time all 3SUB sets had been augmented with a wider steel bodied coach of Bulleid design. On Derby Day in 1952 there were 202 train movements at the station. (J.H.Aston)

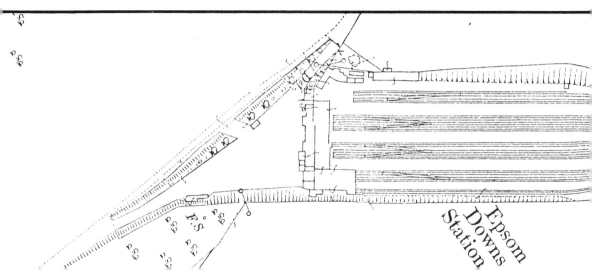

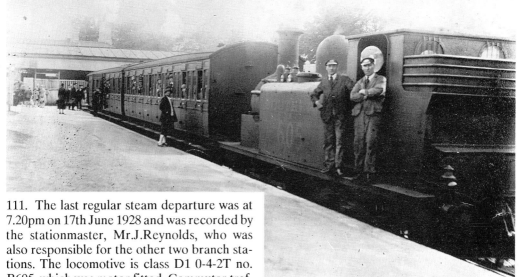

111. The last regular steam departure was at 7.20pm on 17th June 1928 and was recorded by the stationmaster, Mr.J.Reynolds, who was also responsible for the other two branch stations. The locomotive is class D1 0-4-2T no. B605, which was motor fitted. Commuter traffic was slow to develop here, even after electrification, but season tickets on the branch grew from 3000 to 13000 per annum from 1927 to 1933. (J.R.W.Kirkby coll.)

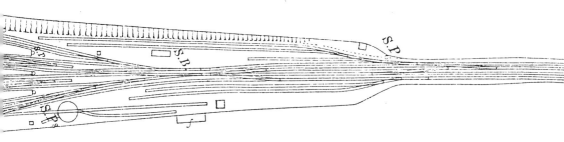

113. Only six of the nine platforms were electrified and five of these were occupied by berthed trains at night in the early years of electrification. The narrow awning at the end of the platforms was removed in the early 1950s, by which time only platforms 3 to 7 had conductor rails. On 1st May 1972 nos. 4 and 5 became 1 and 2, all the other platforms then becoming disused. (Lens of Sutton)

114. There was no goods yard at the station itself but a private siding was situated north of the station on the up side. Originally provided for Mr. Gadsden of North Looe Farm, it was later used by the Kensington & District School. Class C2X is seen with a stores van on 8th June 1957, passing the 1879 iron clad signal box, which was destroyed by fire on 16th November 1981. (J.J.Smith)

115. Platform 2 was the reversal point for the Southern Counties Touring Society on 20th April 1958. The platforms were wholly or partially grass covered intentionally. Only the regularly used areas were surfaced, as can be seen in other views. The station ceased to be a signing-on point for train crews in 1969. (A.E.Bennett)

116. When built, the three doors opened into a large booking hall/general waiting room in which there were doors to first and second class waiting rooms. The two storey house was for the stationmaster and his family. (J.N.Faulkner)

117. A second picture from 13th October 1962 includes a Victoria train (84) and one for London Bridge (39). The last Royal train ran to Epsom Downs in 1924 after which the Royals went by road until after WW2 when they used Tattenham Corner. Pullman, first class and Lord Derby's specials continued to use Epsom Downs until 1939 and Pullmans and first class specials were resumed after the war until 1953. Tattenham Corner station was more conveniently situated to the race course. It did not open until 1901 and so the LBSCR had a monopoly for 35 years. (J.N.Faulkner)

118. The Southern Counties Touring Society had graduated from a two-coach special in 1958 to six coaches and no.34089 *602 Squadron* for "The Surrey Rambler" on 5th June 1966. The notice on the lamppost advises passengers for Banstead and Belmont to use the front four cars only. On the left is the British Rail Staff Association club room. (J.Scrace)

119. A new platform, 300yds nearer Sutton, came into use on 14th February 1989 and is seen in May 1991, by which time it had been fitted with two mirrors for DOO. Up to 1992, the booking office was still staffed in the mornings but the other two on the branch had been closed. (J.Scrace)

120. A mobile temporary booking office was in use while this stylish structure was completed. Photographed in June 1991, a class 455 unit makes an appearance. This occurred only hourly but at least the branch remained open. (S.C.Nash)

MP *Middleton Press*

Easebourne Lane, Midhurst. West Sussex. GU29 9AZ
Tel: (0730) 813169   Fax: (0730) 812601

Write or telephone for our latest booklist

BRANCH LINES

BRANCH LINES TO MIDHURST
BRANCH LINES AROUND MIDHURST
BRANCH LINES TO HORSHAM
BRANCH LINE TO SELSEY
BRANCH LINES TO EAST GRINSTEAD
BRANCH LINES TO ALTON
BRANCH LINE TO TENTERDEN
BRANCH LINES TO NEWPORT
BRANCH LINES TO TUNBRIDGE WELLS
BRANCH LINE TO SWANAGE
BRANCH LINES TO LONGMOOR
BRANCH LINE TO LYME REGIS
BRANCH LINE TO FAIRFORD
BRANCH LINE TO ALLHALLOWS
BRANCH LINES AROUND ASCOT
BRANCH LINES AROUND WEYMOUTH
BRANCH LINE TO HAWKHURST
BRANCH LINES AROUND EFFINGHAM JN
BRANCH LINE TO MINEHEAD
BRANCH LINE TO SHREWSBURY
BRANCH LINES AROUND HUNTINGDON
BRANCH LINES TO SEATON AND SIDMOUTH
BRANCH LINES AROUND WIMBORNE
BRANCH LINES TO EXMOUTH
BRANCH LINE TO LYNTON
BRANCH LINE TO SOUTHWOLD

SOUTH COAST RAILWAYS

BRIGHTON TO WORTHING
CHICHESTER TO PORTSMOUTH
BRIGHTON TO EASTBOURNE
RYDE TO VENTNOR
EASTBOURNE TO HASTINGS
HASTINGS TO ASHFORD
SOUTHAMPTON TO BOURNEMOUTH
ASHFORD TO DOVER
BOURNEMOUTH TO WEYMOUTH
DOVER TO RAMSGATE

COUNTRY RAILWAY ROUTES

BOURNEMOUTH TO EVERCREECH JN
READING TO GUILDFORD
WOKING TO ALTON
BATH TO EVERCREECH JUNCTION
GUILDFORD TO REDHILL
EAST KENT LIGHT RAILWAY
FAREHAM TO SALISBURY
BURNHAM TO EVERCREECH JUNCTION
REDHILL TO ASHFORD
YEOVIL TO DORCHESTER
ANDOVER TO SOUTHAMPTON

SOUTHERN MAIN LINES

HAYWARDS HEATH TO SEAFORD
EPSOM TO HORSHAM
CRAWLEY TO LITTLEHAMPTON
THREE BRIDGES TO BRIGHTON
WATERLOO TO WOKING
VICTORIA TO EAST CROYDON
EAST CROYDON TO THREE BRIDGES
WOKING TO SOUTHAMPTON
WATERLOO TO WINDSOR
LONDON BRIDGE TO EAST CROYDON
BASINGSTOKE TO SALISBURY
SITTINGBOURNE TO RAMSGATE
YEOVIL TO EXETER
CHARING CROSS TO ORPINGTON
VICTORIA TO BROMLEY SOUTH
ORPINGTON TO TONBRIDGE
FAVERSHAM TO DOVER
SALISBURY TO YEOVIL

LONDON SUBURBAN RAILWAYS

CHARING CROSS TO DARTFORD
HOLBORN VIADUCT TO LEWISHAM
KINGSTON & HOUNSLOW LOOPS
CRYSTAL PALACE AND CATFORD LOOP
LEWISHAM TO DARTFORD
MITCHAM JUNCTION LINES

STEAMING THROUGH

STEAMING THROUGH EAST HANTS
STEAMING THROUGH SURREY
STEAMING THROUGH WEST SUSSEX
STEAMING THROUGH THE ISLE OF WIGHT
STEAMING THROUGH WEST HANTS

OTHER BOOKS

GARRAWAY FATHER & SON
LONDON CHATHAM & DOVER RAILWAY
INDUSTRIAL RAILWAYS OF THE S. EAST
WEST SUSSEX RAILWAYS IN THE 1980s
SOUTH EASTERN RAILWAY
TILLINGBOURNE BUS STORY
MILITARY DEFENCE OF WEST SUSSEX
BATTLE OVER PORTSMOUTH
BATTLE OVER SUSSEX 1940
SURREY WATERWAYS
KENT AND EAST SUSSEX WATERWAYS
HAMPSHIRE WATERWAYS
LEIGH PARK
BRIGHTON'S TRAMWAYS
EAST GRINSTEAD THEN & NOW